# SUCCESSFUL AMERICANS

# Americans of South American Heritage

Karen Schweitzer

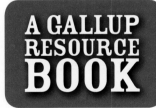

A GALLUP
RESOURCE
BOOK

**Mason Crest Publishers**

**Philadelphia**

Produced by OTTN Publishing in association with
Bow Publications, Inc.

MASON CREST PUBLISHERS INC.
370 Reed Road
Broomall, Pennsylvania 19008
(866) MCP-BOOK (toll free)
www.masoncrest.com

Printed in the United States of America.

First Printing

9 8 7 6 5 4 3 2 1

Library of Congress Cataloging-in-Publication Data

Schweitzer, Karen.
  Americans of South American heritage / Karen Schweitzer.
     p. cm. — (Successful Americans)
  Includes bibliographical references and index.
  ISBN 978-1-4222-0526-6 (hardcover)
  ISBN 978-1-4222-0861-8 (pbk.)
  1. Hispanic Americans—Biography—Juvenile literature.  2. Successful people—
United States—Biography—Juvenile literature.  I. Title.
  E184.S75S285 2009
  305.868'0730922—dc22
  [B]
                                                                    2008042823

Publisher's note:
All quotations in this book come from original sources, and contain the spelling
and grammatical inconsistencies of the original text.

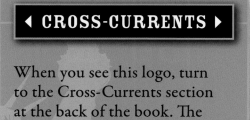

◀ **CROSS-CURRENTS** ▶

When you see this logo, turn
to the Cross-Currents section
at the back of the book. The
Cross-Currents features explore
connections between people,
places, events, and ideas.

# Table of Contents

*South American soccer players compete on the field in the United States.*

## CHAPTER ONE

# Migrating to the North

According to the U.S. Census Bureau, the United States is home to approximately 2.5 million people who were born in South America. Nearly 25 percent of them were born in Colombia. Ecuadorians make up the second largest group of people living in the United States, and Peruvians constitute the third largest. Brazil also accounts for a large segment of the South American immigrant population in the United States. In addition, the country is home to a large group of people who are U.S. born but who, as the children of immigrant parents or grandparents, claim South American ancestry.

## AN OVERVIEW OF SOUTH AMERICAN IMMIGRATION

South Americans have been immigrating to the United States since the early 1800s. When immigration first began, there were very few people who moved from South America to the United States. Today, things are much different.

Government statistics of the number of people emigrating each decade from South America and settling in the United States show a continuing increase over the course of the 20th century. Between 1900 and 1909, just over 15,000 South Americans immigrated to the United States. Two decades later, that number had more than doubled, increasing to 43,000. From 1990 to 1999, nearly 600,000 people moved to the United States from South America.

During the first years of the 21st century, immigration levels have continued to rise. In 2007 alone, more than 100,000 people left South America for

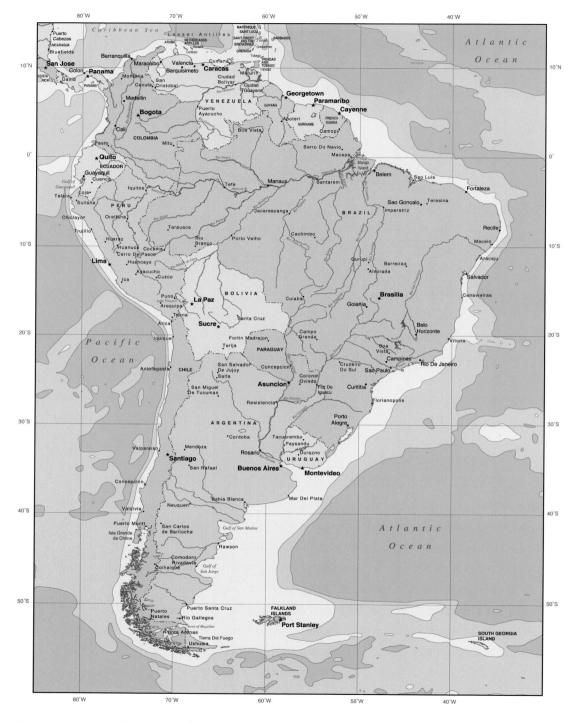

Beginning in the early 1500s South America was colonized by the European nations of Spain and Portugal. Today, the languages of those two countries are the official languages of most of the continent, which is home to more than 370 million people.

0       500 Miles

0       500 KM

Parallel scale at 20°S 0°E

## SOUTH AMERICAN IMMIGRATION BY DECADE

| Decade | Number Arriving in the United States |
|---|---|
| 1900–1909 | 15,253 |
| 1910–1919 | 39,938 |
| 1920–1929 | 43,025 |
| 1930–1939 | 9,990 |
| 1940–1949 | 19,662 |
| 1950–1959 | 78,418 |
| 1960–1969 | 250,754 |
| 1970–1979 | 273,608 |
| 1980–1989 | 399,482 |
| 1990–1999 | 570,624 |
| 2000–2007 | 659,056 |

Source: *2007 Yearbook of Immigration Statistics*

the United States. Some statisticians predict that if immigration levels continue to climb at the same rate, more than 1 million new emigrants from South America will enter the country in the decade of 2011 to 2020.

However, the actual level of immigration to the United States is higher than the official numbers show. The official numbers do not include the number of people who entered the country illegally. An estimated half a million immigrants enter the country each year without U.S. government approval. In 2008, officials at the Pew Hispanic Center, a research organization based in Washington, D.C., estimated that about 12 million illegal immigrants were residing permanently in the country. Some statisticians estimate

### ◀ CROSS-CURRENTS ▶

To see how Gallup polls have reported Americans' changing opinions about overall immigration to the United States, turn to page 51.

## HISPANIC AMERICANS

Hispanic Americans are U.S. citizens who can trace their roots back to Mexico, Spain, and the Spanish-speaking nations of South America, Central America, and the Caribbean. The U.S. Census Bureau estimates that Hispanics account for 15 percent of the total population in the United States. By the year 2050, that number is expected to increase to 24 percent.

that about 8 percent of these illegal immigrants came from South America.

## WHY IMMIGRATE?

There are many reasons why people leave the land of their birth to make a home in a new country. Some people immigrate to find new jobs or educational opportunities for themselves and their families. Others move to escape violence, harsh governments, or poverty. Sometimes natural disasters, such as earthquakes and floods, force people to leave their homeland.

Unstable political situations and poverty caused a sharp increase in emigration from South America during the 1960s. In that decade more than 250,000 people legally immigrated to the United States—more than double the amount of the previous decade. The numbers remained high in the 1970s, due in part to political violence in Chile. In 1973 a harsh military dictatorship took over the country, forcing many Chileans into exile.

War and natural disasters led to increased emigration from several South American countries during the 1980s. A bloody civil war in Peru caused its citizens to flee to other countries. Floods and a devastating earthquake in Ecuador in 1987 forced many people to leave.

During the 1990s a large number of people from Ecuador, Argentina, Peru, and Brazil migrated north because of extreme poverty and economic troubles in their homeland. Many of them left South America in hopes of finding a better life in the United States.

In the United States today, more South American immigrants hail from Colombia than from any other nation on the continent. For several decades that country has endured armed conflict as the established government has battled insurgent groups and violent drug cartels. Years of violence and kidnappings have led many Colombians to leave and resettle in other countries, including the United States.

The desire to migrate varies among residents of South American countries, a 2008 Gallup poll reported. In Venezuela and

## FOREIGN-BORN POPULATION FROM SOUTH AMERICA

| Place of Birth | Number of People Living in the United States |
| --- | --- |
| Argentina | 165,850 |
| Bolivia | 73,394 |
| Brazil | 342,555 |
| Chile | 89,060 |
| Colombia | 592,436 |
| Ecuador | 384,677 |
| Guyana | 250,178 |
| Peru | 382,153 |
| Uruguay | 49,517 |
| Venezuela | 162,524 |
| Other SouthAmerican countries | 50,170 |
| **Total:** | **2,542,514** |

Source: Place of Birth for the Foreign-born Population; U.S. Census Bureau, 2006 American Community Survey.

Migrating to the North

Brazil, for example, fewer than 20 percent of respondents said they would like to emigrate, while around 60 percent would leave Guyana. The Gallup Organization found that an average of 24 percent of residents of Latin American countries would move permanently if they could. (Latin America refers to the parts of the Americas where the national language is Latin-based, especially Spanish and Portuguese. It includes Mexico and countries in Central America and South America.) Of those who wanted

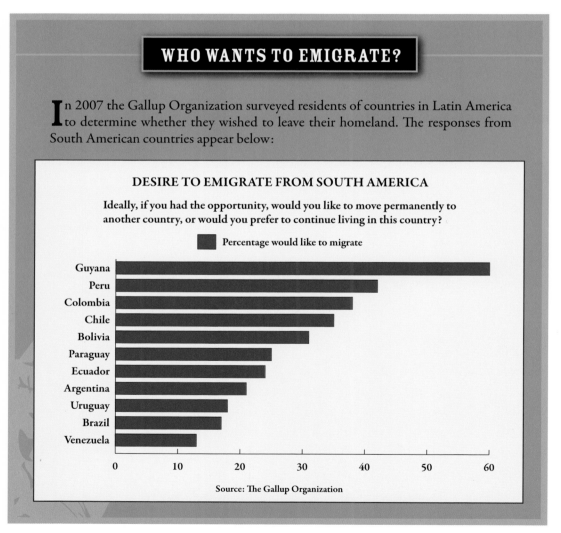

## WHO WANTS TO EMIGRATE?

In 2007 the Gallup Organization surveyed residents of countries in Latin America to determine whether they wished to leave their homeland. The responses from South American countries appear below:

### DESIRE TO EMIGRATE FROM SOUTH AMERICA

Ideally, if you had the opportunity, would you like to move permanently to another country, or would you prefer to continue living in this country?

■ Percentage would like to migrate

|  | |
|---|---|
| Guyana | 60 |
| Peru | 42 |
| Colombia | 38 |
| Chile | 35 |
| Bolivia | 31 |
| Paraguay | 25 |
| Ecuador | 24 |
| Argentina | 21 |
| Uruguay | 18 |
| Brazil | 17 |
| Venezuela | 13 |

Source: The Gallup Organization

to emigrate, the United States was the most popular choice as the final destination.

## ASSIMILATION

Assimilation refers to the process of becoming part of a society or culture. When people immigrating to the United States speak a different language, it becomes more difficult to assimilate.

Many immigrants come the United States knowing little English. According to the U.S. Census Bureau, almost one in five people in the United States speak a language other than English at home. Spanish is the most common language, with more than 28 million people reporting Spanish as the household language. Just over half of these Spanish speakers reported in the 2000 Census that they also speak English "very well."

Those who do not speak English well recognize the importance of learning the language in order to do business, attend school, communicate with doctors, and accomplish day-to-day activities in the United States. Some people believe strongly that Hispanic immigrants need to learn how to speak English, but not lose the language that links them to their Latin culture. Studies have found that by the second and third generations, most immigrant families—including Spanish speakers—have replaced their "home country" language with English.

## COMMUNITIES

Many immigrants from South America have settled in communities in which members share similar backgrounds, culture, and language. The largest communities of South American immigrants can typically be found in big cities.

According to the U.S. Census Bureau, more than 90 percent of South American–born immigrants make their homes in cities that have a population of at least one million. The majority (about 40 percent) live in the New York City metropolitan

*The nighttime skyline of Miami. Located in southeastern Florida, Miami contains a large South American immigrant population.*

area, which includes parts of the states of New York, New Jersey, and Pennsylvania. More than 20 percent of South Americans who immigrate to the United States settle in Florida, especially in the cities of Miami, Fort Lauderdale, and Pompano Beach. Some other cities with high concentrations of people of South American ancestry include Washington, D.C., and Los Angeles, California.

## CHAPTER TWO

# Cesar Pelli: Award-winning Architect

A rgentina-born Cesar Pelli is widely considered to be one of the most influential and accomplished architects in America. He has designed buildings and landmarks built in countries all over the world. His works, which have won more than a hundred awards, highlight the skylines of cities like London, New York, and Tokyo.

Many of Pelli's designs have been called masterpieces, but he doesn't see them that way. He explains, "I don't feel I'm building masterpieces. If a building is a masterpiece, that happens after the fact."

## EARLY INFLUENCES

Cesar Pelli was born on October 12, 1926, in San Miguel de Tucumán, the largest city in northern Argentina. His mother was a Criollo—a descendant of the people who were born in Spanish colonies. His father was the son of an Italian immigrant, who

*Cesar Pelli emigrated from Argentina in 1952 to the United States, where he established a successful architectural firm.*

## ARGENTINA

The nation of Argentina is located in southern South America. It borders the Atlantic Ocean, between Chile and Uruguay and is the second-largest country in South America, after Brazil. More than 40 million people live in Argentina. Most are descended from Spanish and Italian immigrants. The official language of the country is Spanish.

passed on to his grandson a love of marble and other materials common in his native Italy.

As an architect Pelli would include these natural elements in his designs. He would also be influenced by the city in which he grew up. San Miguel de Tucumán, often known simply as Tucumán, is an old Latin American city that is nestled in the side of the Aconquija Mountains. It is famous for its Spanish colonial houses, red tile roofs, and tropical gardens.

The National University of Tucumán, where Pelli studied architecture, was well known. During the 1940s, architecture students from all over Latin America attended this university to study under its famous professors.

## A NEW WORLD

Pelli earned an architecture degree from the National University of Tucumán in 1949. The following year he married fellow student Diana Balmori. She was an accomplished designer, specializing in landscape and urban designs. Together, they had two children, Denis and Rafael.

In 1952 the Pellis moved to the United States so that Cesar could continue his studies at the University of Illinois at Urbana-Champaign. Two years later he earned his master's degree in architecture.

After graduation Pelli was hired by Eero Saarinen, a highly regarded Finnish-American architect known for his unorthodox designs. Pelli worked at Eero's firm, Eero Saarinen and Associates, in Bloomfield Hills, Michigan, for the next 10 years. During that time, he took part in a number of project designs, including the Morse and Stiles Colleges (1961) at Yale University and the TWA Flight Center (1962) at New York's John F. Kennedy Airport.

In 1964 Pelli became a naturalized citizen. That same year he left Eero's firm and went to work for Daniel, Mann, Johnson, and Mendenhall (DNJM) in Los Angeles. He remained in Los Angeles but changed jobs, joining Gruen Associates in 1968 as an associate architect. The position describes an architect who has an employment agreement or a temporary partnership with another architect. As an associate architect, Pelli completed several major assignments over the next eight years. His projects included the prize-winning City Hall in San Bernardino, California (1969), and the Embassy of the United States in Tokyo, Japan (1972).

◀ CROSS-CURRENTS ▶

Cesar Pelli's son, Rafael grew up to be an architect like his father. To learn more about him and how he specializes in "green architecture," turn to page 52.

## CESAR PELLI AND ASSOCIATES

In 1977 Pelli moved to Connecticut to start his own architecture firm—Cesar Pelli and Associates. He also had accepted the job of Dean of the School of Architecture at Yale University, in New Haven. Not long after, he was asked to renovate the Museum of Modern Art (MOMA) in New York City. There were many other architects competing for the job, but Pelli made the final cut. The decision was unexpected, he would later say: "I came east without a [design] job, without connections, without a client, nothing. My intention was to be a teacher—and maybe do kitchen additions. A month after I started as dean, I got a call about MOMA."

Pelli had been selected to design a new west wing for the museum. He called on his wife, Diana, and his friend and colleague Fred Clarke to help. The major renovation, which doubled the gallery exhibit space, added a new film theater, and included a glass-enclosed garden hall, was completed in 1984.

Pelli never did do kitchen additions, but he was asked to design many other buildings over the years, including the World Financial Center complex (1981–1987) in downtown Manhattan. In 1984 Pelli resigned from his position at Yale so that he could concentrate on his firm full-time.

That decision paid off. By 1990 there were more than 80 North American, Latin American, European, and Japanese architects working for Cesar Pelli and Associates. Pelli was involved in every project they worked on and continued to build his reputation as a brilliant architect.

In 1991 Pelli was selected as one of the ten most influential living American architects by the American Institute of Architects. A few years later, in 1995, the same organization awarded him its coveted AIA Gold Medal. This award is given

*Among Pelli's most famous designs are the west wing and residential tower of New York City's Museum of Modern Art (left) and the Petronas Twin Towers (right), in Kuala Lumpur, Malaysia.*

*Pelli participates in the groundbreaking ceremony for the Red Building, the final structure of three office buildings designed for the Pacific Design Center complex, in West Hollywood, California.*

in recognition of a significant body of work in the theory and practice of architecture.

## A WORLDWIDE INFLUENCE

Pelli's works have earned him the respect of his peers as well as many awards. And his designs have influenced urban landscapes all over the world.

Many Pelli projects are among the tallest buildings in the world. One major project was the 88-floor Petronas Twin Towers (1998), located in Kuala Lumpur, Malaysia. The structures are the tallest twin buildings in the world. Pelli also contributed to the design of the Goldman Sachs Tower (2004), in Jersey City, New Jersey. Another tall building is the 25 Bank Street Skyscraper, which is the eighth-tallest building in Canary Wharf, London.

To recognize the increased role of architects Fred Clarke and Rafael Pelli in Cesar Pelli's firm, the company was renamed Pelli Clarke Pelli Architects in 2005. The firm continues to design award-winning projects that include major public spaces, museums, airports, performing arts centers, hotels, and office and residential towers in countries around the world.

## CHAPTER THREE

# Isabel Allende: Novelist

Isabel Allende is one of the most recognized Latin American writers in the world. She has worked as a journalist, a literature professor, and an author. And she has been recognized with literary awards and honorary degrees from more than a dozen respected universities. Much of her writing has been inspired by the political and social issues that exist in South America.

## THE EARLY YEARS

Isabel Allende was born in Lima, Peru, on August 2, 1942. Her father, Tomás Allende, was a diplomatic official and citizen of Chile, as well as the cousin of Salvador Allende, who would later become the country's president. Isabel's mother, Francisca Llona Allende, was the daughter of Chilean citizens Isabel Barros Moreira and Agustin Llona Cuevas.

When Isabel was three years old, her father left the family, which was still living in Peru. Francisca Llona returned to Chile,

*In 1988 novelist Isabel Allende, a political refugee from Chile, came to the United States.*

## CHILE

The nation of Chile is located in southern South America. The long strip of land that makes up the country borders the South Pacific Ocean, between Argentina and Peru. More than 16 million people live in Chile.

taking Isabel and her two brothers to live with their maternal grandparents in Santiago, the capital city of Chile.

While Isabel was still a child, her mother married another diplomat, Ramón Huidobro. An employee for the Ministry of Foreign Affairs, Huidobro was sent to La Paz, Bolivia, in the early 1950s. There, Isabel and her siblings were enrolled in a private school. Later, the family relocated again to Beirut, Lebanon.

Moving so much and living in different countries was difficult for Isabel. In her memoir, *My Invented Country* (2003), she described her feelings:

> From the moment we left Chile and began to travel from country to country, I became the new girl in the neighborhood, the foreigner at school, the strange one who dressed differently and didn't even know how to talk like everyone else.

## RETURN TO CHILE

In 1958, when Isabel was 15 years old, she and her brothers returned to Chile. They moved back into their grandfather's home in Santiago, where they completed their schooling. That same year, Isabel met Miguel Frias, an engineering student. The two married four years later. They had two children, Paula, born in 1963, and Nicolas, born in 1966.

During the 1960s Isabel worked as a secretary and was also responsible for looking after the children and running the house. She later landed work as an editor and journalist, employed by a woman's magazine called *Paula* and a children's magazine called *Mampato*. She also worked as a talk show television host.

## POLITICAL REFUGEE

Isabel's life changed forever on September 11, 1973, when the Chilean military, with the help of the U.S. Central Intelligence Agency (CIA), overthrew Chilean president Salvador Allende. The military government reported that Salvador committed suicide, but it is widely believed that he was assassinated on the order of General Augusto Pinochet Ugarte, who led the coup and later declared himself president.

*A photograph of Allende taken September 1974 in Helsinki, Finland, where she was attending an anti-coup demonstration.*

After Pinochet began ordering Allende supporters to be rounded up, tortured, and killed, Isabel helped many people find safe passage out of the country. But when her name was added to the wanted list she was forced to take her family and flee to Caracas, Venezuela.

Up until the military coup Isabel had not been politically active. As a refugee in Venezuela, she was more conscious of political and social issues. During her exile she also came to realize how important Salvador Allende, who had been a democratically elected president, was to the rest of the world:

> After the military coup, I realized that he had a historical dimension. I only saw that after I left Chile, because after the coup, when I was in Chile, his name was banned. When I went to Venezuela, every time I said my name,

people would ask immediately if I was related to Salvador Allende. Then I realized what a man he was. He has become a legendary figure, a hero.

## FROM REFUGEE TO AUTHOR

In Caracas Isabel continued to work as a freelance journalist. But she found it difficult to get work. She turned to writing novels, drawing on her experiences and on the brutal events of 1973.

Allende's first novel, *La Casa de los Espiritos* (*The House of the Spirits*), was published in Spanish in 1982. It became a best-seller and was soon translated into English for publication in the United States. Subsequent books included *Of Love and Shadows* (1984) and *Eva Luna* (1985).

Isabel divorced her husband in 1987. During a trip to the United States, she met and fell in love with an American attorney named William "Willie" Gordon. They married in July 1988, and Isabel moved to a new home in San Rafael, north of San Francisco, California. Among the books the author subsequently produced were *Stories of Eva Luna*, in 1989, and *The Infinite Plan*, in 1991.

## MOURNING THE LOSS OF A DAUGHTER

In 1991 Isabel's daughter Paula fell ill with a hormonal disorder called porphyria. The disease left her in a coma and she died six months later from complications.

While her daughter lay ill, Isabel talked to her. The author told stories about her childhood, her thoughts as a writer, and her exile in Venezuela. After Paula's death in 1992, Isabel wrote down those stories in the form of a letter to her daughter. The

◄ **CROSS-CURRENTS** ►

Salvador Allende was the first democratically elected socialist president of Chile. U.S. officials sought to destabilize his government because they did not agree with his policies. For more information about the Chilean coup of 1973, turn to page 52.

resulting book, published in 1995, was called *Paula*. The process of writing the memoir helped her to mourn, she explained later: "That book was written with tears, but it was very healing tears. After it was finished, I felt that my daughter was alive in my heart, her memory preserved. As long as it is written, it will be remembered."

*Chilean president Michelle Bachelet receives a copy of Allende's novel* Ines of My Soul. *The novel tells the story of Ines de Suarez, the wife of the Spanish conqueror Pedro de Valdivia, the founder of the Chilean capital city of Santiago.*

## LITERARY LEGEND

In addition to writing, Allende has also worked as a college professor. She has taught literature at several schools in the United States, including Montclair State College, in Montclair, New Jersey; the University of Virginia, in Charlottesville; and the University of California, in Berkeley. Allende's accomplishments

have led to many international literary awards, including the Independent Foreign Fiction Award, the Dorothy and Lillian Gish Prize, and the Books to Remember Award.

Isabel Allende did not return to Chile until General Augusto Pinochet was overthrown in 1989. At that time she returned briefly to celebrate the country's likely return to democracy. But she also noted that she considered her home to be in California. The first freely elected president of Chile took office in 1990. Sixteen years later the first woman president of the country, Michelle Bachelet was elected.

Allende obtained her U.S. citizenship in 2003. However, she remains true to her Latin roots. She visits Chile three or four times a year. And in 2006 she represented the continent of South America as a flag bearer at the Opening Ceremony of the Winter Olympics. In 2007 she was named the third most influential Latino leader in the world by *Latino Leaders* magazine.

## CHAPTER FOUR

# Benjamin Bratt: Actor

The son of a Quechua Peruvian Indian, Benjamin Bratt has worked as a professional actor for more than 20 years. The American-born actor has appeared in more than 40 movies and television shows. He has won major awards for his work and has been nominated for many others. When he's not acting Bratt devotes the majority of his time to his family and to Native American causes.

*Actor Benjamin Bratt claims ancestry from Peru and Germany.*

## FAMILY ROOTS

Benjamin's mother, Eldy Banda, was born in Lima, Peru, in 1937. Lima is the largest city in Peru and the 19th most populous city in the world. At the age of 14 Eldy left Lima and immigrated to the United States. She lived with her grandmother, who worked for a wealthy American family. After her grandmother died, Eldy was adopted by the family. She eventually met and married Peter Bratt, an American man of English and German descent.

On December 16, 1963, Benjamin Bratt was born to the couple in San Francisco, California. He would be the middle child in a family of five children. He had an older sister and a brother and soon had two more sisters. But in 1968, when Benjamin was four years old, his parents divorced. Eldy, who was a registered nurse, raised him and his four siblings by herself.

The Bratt family didn't have a lot of money, but they did have a close relationship with one another. The kids were taught to be proud of their heritage. According to Benjamin, Eldy often talked to them about her homeland and her Quechuan roots. He told an interviewer:

> She made us aware at a very early age of the indigenous aspect of her culture. And this was in fact uncommon at the time because, even today, there's such a great prejudice in South America against the indigenous culture that people are afraid to admit that they're part native. To call someone an "indio" is still an insult.

### ◀ CROSS-CURRENTS ▶

To learn more about Benjamin's mother, Eldy Banda, who participated in the Native American movement during the 1970s, turn to page 53.

## ACTOR IN TRAINING

As a teenager Benjamin attended Lowell High School in San Francisco, California. He was outgoing and participated in a number of school activities, including the Lowell Forensic Society. This high school group, founded in 1892, is the oldest debate team in the United States. Its members travel all over the country to participate in speech and debate tournaments.

After graduating from high school in 1982, Benjamin enrolled at the University of California at Santa Barbara. While in college he decided to pursue acting as a career. Four years later, he had obtained a bachelor of fine arts degree, graduating with honors in 1986. The next step was further study at the American Conservatory Theatre, in San Francisco, where he had been accepted for a master's degree program.

In order to pay the school's tuition, Bratt drove vans to and from the San Francisco International Airport. However, he did not complete the degree. In 1987 he decided to quit after being offered a starring role on a new television series called *Juarez and Lovers*.

## WORKING ACTOR

Although a pilot was filmed, *Juarez and Lovers* never aired on television. However, Bratt continued to audition for movies and television shows. In 1988 he made his small screen debut in the TV movie *Police Story: Gladiator School*. Other roles soon followed. Between 1988 and 1990 Benjamin appeared in two different television shows, *Knightwatch* and *Nasty Boys*. Both shows were cancelled after a few episodes.

Over the next several years, Benjamin appeared in a string of Hollywood movies. The first was *One Good Cop* (1991), starring Michael Keaton and Rene Russo. The second was *Demolition Man* (1993), starring Wesley Snipes and Sylvester Stallone. The parts Benjamin played in both movies were small.

Most of the films Bratt appeared in met with little fanfare. However, he did gain attention for his role as a Native American forest ranger in the movie *The River Wild* (1994).

## LAW AND ORDER

Bratt's big break came in 1995, when he was offered a recurring role on the popular television drama *Law and Order*. He was asked to play Reynaldo "Rey" Curtis, a homicide detective who likes to do things by the book. Benjamin accepted the role and became a household name within months.

In 1996 Bratt acted in the movie *Follow Me Home*, which was directed by his brother, Peter Bratt. The film explores the relationships among four artists of different races—one black, one

*In November 2007 Bratt and his wife, Talisa Soto, pose at the Los Angeles premiere for the film* Love in the Time of Cholera, *in which he starred. The movie is based on the award-winning novel by Colombian author Gabriel Garcia Márquez.*

Native American, and two Latin Americans. Critics gave Benjamin and the film good reviews. The movie went on to win the Best Feature Film Audience Award at the 1996 San Francisco International Film Festival.

## FAMILY MAN

In 1999 Bratt made the difficult decision to leave *Law and Order*. Although he loved working on the show, he said, he missed seeing his family on a regular basis. His mother, brother, and three sisters still lived in California. *Law and Order* was filmed in New York.

After leaving the television show, Bratt moved to San Francisco and concentrated on making movies. Between 2000 and 2002, he appeared in seven different films, including the award-winning *Traffic* (2000) and the box office hit *Miss Congeniality* (2000).

In April 2002 Benjamin married actress Talisa Soto. The couple had their first child, a girl named Sophia Rosalinda Bratt, the following December. Their second child, a boy named Mateo Bravery Bratt, was born in October 2005.

Bratt has continued to make movies, acting in at least one film every year. In 2008 he signed on to star in an A&E television series called *The Cleaner*. In the program he plays a former drug addict who helps other people overcome their addictions. Both Bratt and the show have received good reviews from critics and fans alike.

## CHAPTER FIVE

# Bob Burnquist: Pro Skateboarder

**M**any people regard Bob Burnquist as one of the most talented and creative skateboarders in the world. He has been skating professionally since the age of 15. Over the years, the Brazilian-born skateboarder has won various awards and contests, but he is best known for the death-defying stunts he performs.

## GROWING UP IN BRAZIL

Bob Dean Silva Burnquist was born in Rio de Janeiro, Brazil, on October 10, 1976, to an American father and a Brazilian mother—Dora Burnquist. He grew up in Sao Paulo, the largest city in Brazil, which has a population of about 27 million people.

Although most people who live in Sao Paulo are of Italian descent, the official language of Brazil is Portuguese. So Bob and his two sisters grew up speaking

*Skateboarder Bob Burnquist shows off his skills at the Bowl-A-Rama in Sydney, Australia, in February 2007.*

## BRAZIL

The largest and most populous country in South America, Brazil is located in the eastern part of the continent. The nation borders the Atlantic Ocean and shares boundaries with every South American country except Chile and Ecuador. The population of Brazil is almost 200 million. Portuguese is the official language.

Portuguese. They learned some English at home and even more in a private school.

Bob has told interviewers that he had trouble dealing with the fact that his family was wealthy enough to send him to private school while so many other people in Sao Paulo were poor. He explains: "There's a wide gap between the rich and the poor. I saw a lot of street kids and homeless people. I was like, 'Why do I get to go to school and they don't?' I didn't understand it, and I tried to run away from reality."

The comment about running "away from reality" refers to the dangerous habit of sniffing glue that Burnquist developed as a child. Such substance abuse can lead to hearing loss, brain damage, and in some cases, death. Burnquist dropped the dangerous habit before it became an addiction—or worse. "Skateboarding snapped me out of that," he says. "[The sport] saved my life."

## PRO BOARDER

Burnquist became a skateboarder at the age of 10. Soon he was skating every moment that he wasn't in school. Within a matter of months, he was competing in skateboarding contests in Brazil—and winning them. In 1992, at age 15, he turned pro.

Bob says it was easy going from an amateur (am) to a professional (pro) skateboarder. He told an interviewer:

> One thing led to the next and before I knew it, I was getting paid to skate. Turning pro wasn't a big formality—it was actually kind of funny. I skated a couple open pro/am contests in Brazil and qualified in the first one. In the second one, I just told the announcer that I was pro now.

Burnquist continued to skate for fun and for money. He often practiced at the skate park that was near his house. When that closed down, he began to skate on all sorts of different terrains throughout Brazil. The street and cement bowls were Bob's favorite places to practice.

By 1994 Burnquist had developed a reputation as an innovative boarder who had the ability to perform tricks both backward and forward. In the spring of that year, reporters from *Thrasher,* a popular skateboarding magazine, visited Brazil to learn more about the young skateboarder. They were impressed by what they saw and encouraged Burnquist to come to the United States to try his skills in a new land.

## MOVING TO THE UNITED STATES

Bob visited San Francisco in 1994. While there, he got a new American-made board and other skateboarding equipment. The following year he entered and won his first North American pro contest—the Slam City Jam in Vancouver, Canada.

Winning the contest changed Bob's life. He made the decision to move to the United States and began competing in skateboarding full-time. He continued to compete in Brazil, and won many of the competitions he entered there and in the United States.

◄ **CROSS-CURRENTS** ►

Burnquist is a citizen of the United States and Brazil. To learn more about dual citizenship, turn to page 53.

One of Bob's most exciting wins came at the X Games—the annual extreme action sports competition that features skateboarding and motorsports. At the 2001 games, held in Philadelphia, Pennsylvania, he competed in the Skateboard Vert. This X Games event takes place on a half-pipe that goes from a flat surface to a vertical wall. Burnquist received a score of 98—the highest point average ever seen at a skateboarding competition.

From 2002 to 2008 Burnquist has taken first place or won gold at an impressive number of contests, including the OP King of Skate and the Vans Triple Crown. Bob has also won a dozen X Games medals. He appears in the skateboarding video games *Tony Hawk Pro Skater* and *ESPN X Games Skateboarding* as a playable character.

*Burnquist celebrates winning another gold medal for Skateboard Vert Best Trick at the 2005 X Games, held at the Staples Center in Los Angeles.*

In 2000 Bob became a father when his girlfriend and pro skateboarder Jen O'Brien gave birth to their daughter Lotus. In 2007 Bob became a father once again when Brazilian girlfriend Veronica Nachard gave birth to their daughter Jasmyn.

## GOING GREEN

Bob is more than just a professional skateboarder. He participates in a number of skateboarding projects and is very active in the Action Sports Environment Coalition (ASEC). The ASEC is a nonprofit organization whose members include many extreme sports athletes. The group works to educate people about the environment and global warming. ASEC has a strong interest in the environment

*Burnquist and fellow skater Jennifer O'Brien make an appearance with their daughter Lotus at a 2004 fundraiser benefiting Standup for Skateparks. The event helped raise money for the Tony Hawk Foundation, which supports programs to create public skate parks for kids.*

because its members make their living in outdoor sports (such as skateboarding, skiing, and motocross cycling).

At his home outside San Diego, California, Burnquist has a backyard for skateboarding, complete with a mega-ramp, vert ramp, and full pipe. But the site is also the location of his organic farm—Burnquist Organics. He promotes healthy eating habits through the Bob Burnquist Foundation, which is dedicated to teaching about good food and organic gardening.

Whatever else Bob does in the future, he says one thing is certain—he will continue to skate:

> I'll probably be on my board as long as I can, but I don't know about skating professionally. The stuff I'm doing, I can already feel in my body. The pounding is going to add up, I know that. I also know that I can't stop doing it. Hopefully, I can extend my professional skateboard life for another twenty years. If I can do that, I'll be very, very happy.

**Bob Burnquist: Pro Skateboarder**

## CHAPTER SIX

# Wilmer Valderrama: Actor and Restaurateur

**W**ilmer Valderrama is an award-winning actor who is of Colombian and Venezuelan ancestry. He has appeared both on television and film. Although he is best known as an actor in the television sitcom *That '70s Show* and in several films, Valderrama has many other talents as well. He heads up a production company and a fashion label, and he owns and operates several popular restaurants.

### GROWING UP IN VENEZUELA

Wilmer Valderrama was born in Miami, Florida, on January 30, 1980, to Balvino and Sobeida Valderrama. He is the oldest of four children. His siblings include two sisters, Marilyn and Stephanie, and one brother, Christian. Wilmer's mother is Colombian and his father is Venezuelan. They met each other in Miami in 1977 while on vacation.

*Actor Wilmer Valderrama knew little English when he came to the United States from Venezuela at age 14.*

## COLOMBIA AND VENEZUELA

**B**oth Colombia and Venezuela are located in northern South America, bordering each other as well as the Caribbean Sea and the North Atlantic Ocean. Colombia also borders the North Pacific Ocean—it is the only South American country with coastlines on both the Pacific and Caribbean. Venezuela has a population of more than 25 million, while more than 45 million people live in Colombia. Spanish is the official language in both countries.

When Wilmer was three years old, his father moved the family to Acarigua-Araure, Venezuela. The large metropolitan city used to be the state capital of Portuguesa, one of Venezuela's 23 states. Acarigua-Araure is still an important commercial area in South America.

Wilmer's dad worked land for farmers. The jobs he got were seasonal and did not pay well. The family was so poor that there were times when they could afford to eat dinner only every other night.

Although things were difficult, Wilmer still found ways to have fun. He was very athletic and enjoyed playing sports. His favorite activities were biking, rollerblading, and soccer. He even learned to ride a unicycle.

In 1994 Balvino Valderrama decided to move his family to the United States. He sold everything he owned so that the Valderramas could afford the journey. Balvino was sure there would be more opportunities for his children in the United States.

## LEARNING ENGLISH

The Valderrama family settled in Los Angeles, California. Wilmer was only 14 years old when he found himself in a country where English was the official spoken language. The young teen had grown up speaking Spanish and wasn't familiar with the English language at all. In hopes of picking up a few words, Wilmer began watching TV shows like *I Love Lucy*.

Wilmer also enrolled in the local school, William Howard Taft High. He would later tell an interviewer how difficult it was adjusting to his new life at school: "Just picture a kid going to the cafeteria, not even knowing how to ask for an orange juice. I would find the loneliest table. I sat there petrified of people who had blue eyes and blond hair."

Valderrama found a way to make the transition from Venezuela to the United States easier for him. In his sophomore year, he joined his high school's drama club. He later said that he thought performing in plays would be a good way for him to practice and improve his English. The plan worked—and it even led to a career.

### THAT '70S SHOW

After being told by his drama teacher that he had talent, Valderrama decided to hire an agent. It wasn't long before he was cast in the CBS television series *Four Corners* and the Disney Channel's *Omba Makamba,* both broadcast in 1998. That year he also landed a role on *That '70s Show* , a new sitcom on the Fox Television Network.

The show featured six teenagers living in 1970s Point Place, Wisconsin. Valderrama was cast as one of the teenagers—a foreign exchange student named Fez who is trying to understand and join the culture of his friends. The show's producers wanted Fez to have a Latin American accent; Wilmer was a natural for the part.

The other actors in *That '70s Show* included Topher Grace, Ashton Kutcher, Danny Masterson, Laura Prepon, and Mila

**◀ CROSS-CURRENTS ▶**

Like many children of immigrants, Wilmer did not speak English when he arrived in the United States. Until he learned the language, classes were difficult. Schools call such students English-language learners, or ELLs. To learn more, turn to page 54.

Kunis. Nearly all of them were unknown actors at the time of the show's debut. But the show was an immediate hit, receiving high ratings from both teenage and adult audiences. Within a few months of its debut, *That '70s Show* was renewed for another season by the Fox Network.

In only four year's time Valderrama had gone from the shy kid who couldn't speak English to a working actor on a popular television show. The new job also provided something he had never had before: financial security. When he was only 18 years old he bought his family a house outside Los Angeles and began to support them. He told an interviewer in 2001 that he didn't mind sharing his success and his money with his family, by explaining, "If it weren't for them. I would never be where I am today."

*The cast of* That '70s Show, *which ran from 1998 to 2006, included (from top, left to right) Mila Kunis, Danny Masterson, Wilmer Valderrama, Ashton Kutcher, Topher Grace, and Laura Prepon.*

**Wilmer Valderrama: Actor and Restaurateur**

## BRANCHING OUT

Between tapings of *That '70s Show* Valderrama broke into the movie business. He made his big screen debut in 2001 in the comedy drama *Summer Catch*, with costars Freddie Prinze, Jr., and Jessica Biel. Valderrama also appeared in the 2003 movie *Party Monster,* starring Macaulay Culkin and Seth Green.

For several years *That '70s Show* continued to do well in the ratings. By 2004 it was being broadcast in countries all over the world. Valderrama's newfound fame and wealth provided many opportunities, and he invested in various projects.

One of the earliest ventures was a Japanese eatery called Geisha House. Valderrama partnered with his costars Ashton Kutcher and Danny Masterson to buy the Hollywood restaurant, as well as a few others. By 2006 he owned three restaurants and had three more in the works.

Valderrama also started a production company called WV Enterprises. One of the company's first projects was a reality television show for MTV called *Yo Momma*. He created the show, a comedy competition, and served as its host and executive producer.

*Yo Momma* premiered on television on April 3, 2006. A month later the final episode of *That '70s Show* aired on the Fox Network. The show remained popular, even in its final season, but the cast was ready to move on to other projects.

## NEW GOALS

Valderrama acted in several more movies. One was the critically acclaimed drama *Fast Food Nation* (2006), which examines negative aspects of the meat packaging industry. Valderrama played an illegal immigrant who finds work in a slaughterhouse. Other films he has appeared in include the crime dramas *Columbus Day* and *Days of Wrath*, both released in 2008. And Wilmer also provides the voice for Manny, the main character on the Disney Channel's preschool series *Handy Manny*.

In August 2007 Valderrama launched a fashion line for men called Calavena. Consisting mostly of jeans, t-shirts, and jackets, the clothing line reflects Wilmer's goal of creating clothing for everyone. He says, "The name Calavena comes from two words, 'calavera' means skull in Spanish and 'vena' is vein. Combined, they're pretty much the original blueprint for any living being."

Valderrama plans to continue acting and producing. In 2008 he signed a deal with Fremantle Media, the coproducer of *American Idol,* to develop scripts for film and television.

*A scene from the 2006 film* Fast Food Nation, *in which Valderrama plays an immigrant who has been smuggled into the United States.*

## CHAPTER SEVEN

# Christina Aguilera: Singer and Songwriter

The daughter of an Ecuadorian father and a mother of Irish descent, Christina Aguilera is an accomplished singer, songwriter, and record producer. She has sold more than 37 million albums worldwide and is considered to be one of the most successful recording artists of the 21st century. When she's not performing, Christina dedicates her time to charities and other philanthropic efforts.

## THE EARLY YEARS

Christina Maria Aguilera was born on December 18, 1980, in Staten Island, New York, to Fausto Wagner Xavier Aguilera and Shelly Loraine Fidler. Fasuto was born in Guayaquil, Ecuador. At the time of Christina's birth, he was a sergeant in the U.S. Army. Shelly was a Spanish interpreter.

*Singer Christina Aguilera performs at the 2008 MTV video music awards.*

## ECUADOR

The country of Ecuador is located in western South America, where it borders the Pacific Ocean at the equator and the nations of Colombia and Peru. About 90 percent of its almost 14 million people are of Amerindian ancestry. Spanish is the official language, although people also speak Quechua.

Christina is the oldest of five children. She has two younger brothers, Casey and Michael, and two younger sisters, Rachel and Stephanie.

Although she was born in New York, Christina didn't stay there very long. Her father's job required the family to move around a lot. During her childhood, she lived in Florida, Texas, New York, and New Jersey. She even spent some time in Japan.

Life wasn't always easy for the young girl. Her father was abusive towards Shelly and the kids. When Christina was six years old, her mother divorced Fausto and took the kids to live with Christina's grandmother in Rochester, Pennsylvania, outside Pittsburgh. They later moved to another Pittsburgh suburb, Wexford.

## LITTLE GIRL WITH A BIG VOICE

Christina began to sing almost as soon as she could talk. She would sing for her family, friends, and even strangers on the street. Her favorite kind of music was soul and blues, but she sang almost anything she could learn the words to. Christina's family recognized her talent early on and encouraged her to follow her dreams of singing.

In 1988 seven-year-old Christina made her first television appearance when she participated in an amateur talent show called *Star Search*. She just missed winning the event, coming in at second place. She also performed at local block parties and sporting events. It wasn't long before the young singer became known as the little girl with the big voice. According to Christina, the reputation didn't help her make friends:

> I constantly felt like an outsider growing up. . . . The other kids weren't very kind to me when my name appeared in the paper or when I was on *Star Search* when I was 7. So I completely relate to anybody that feels that they ever have to confine anything about themselves to please someone else. I knew at a really young age that I would never do that, that I would always be courageous and stand up for what I believed in.

The New Mickey Mouse Club *featured rising stars Justin Timberlake, Britney Spears, and Ryan Gosling, in addition to Christina Aguilera (middle row, right).*

At age 12, Christina won a role on *The New Mickey Mouse Club*. First broadcast in 1989, the popular variety show was produced by Disney Channel. She appeared on the show from 1993 to 1995 with future pop stars Justin Timberlake, Britney Spears, and JC Chasez, as well as future actors Ryan Gosling and Keri Russell.

## RISING STAR

After *The New Mickey Mouse Club* was cancelled Aguilera continued to work hard at developing her music career. At age 14, she and her mother moved to Japan where she recorded her first song. "All I Want to Do," a duet with Japanese pop star Keizo Nakanishi, was an instant hit when it was released in 1995.

Aguilera spent some time touring Japan and other countries with Nakanishi, performing the song in concerts. She became very popular overseas. In fact, she was so popular that she almost caused a riot among 10,000 fans at a rock festival in Romania who wanted to get close to the young star.

By early 1998 Christina was in New York City, where she made a demo tape in order to obtain a recording contract. Her first big break soon came when a Disney Studios rep heard the tape. Disney executives had been looking for someone to sing the song "Reflection" for the movie *Mulan*. Impressed with her talent, they offered her the job.

*Aguilera shows off her Grammy for Best New Artist, received in February 2000.*

That same week Aguilera was offered a record deal with RCA Records. She hesitated accepting the offer, however, when officials at the record company asked her to change her last name of Aguilera to something that sounded "more American." Christina refused.

As it turned out, the last name never became an issue. People were blown away by the self-titled first album. *Christina Aguilera*, released in 1998, earned three Grammy nominations and three number one singles on the Billboard Top 100. The first single, "Genie in a Bottle" sold more than 2 million copies. The album sold more than 8 million. At the 1999 Grammy Awards, Aguilera took home the award for Best New Artist.

Christina's next album, *Mi Reflejo*, was released in September 2000. It led to more hits and worldwide fame. It also earned her a Grammy Award from the Latin Recording Academy.

**◄ CROSS-CURRENTS ►**

The title of Christina's September 2000 album is Spanish for "My Reflection." To find out why the artist had not performed in Spanish before, read about *Mi Reflejo* on page 55.

## SUPERSTAR

A team of songwriters and producers had been behind Aguilera's first studio album. For her second studio recording she decided take complete creative control. Christina cowrote 14 of the songs and even helped produce the album, called *Stripped,* which was released in 2002.

Aguilera later said that she believed *Stripped* was different from her two previous albums because it was much more personal. She explained in an interview:

This album was about me, for the first time, getting to play with all kinds of different sounds and people— you know, making it as personal as I wanted to. What I wanted to do with this record is tell a story. My story. It talks about things that happened with my father and my past, and with a song like "Beautiful," being vulnerable and feeling good about yourself. Or "Fighter," which is about coming out of a hard situation and being able to pick yourself back up.

Aguilera's fans embraced the singer's new, more grown-up sound. *Stripped* sold more than 12 million copies worldwide and produced five commercial singles, including the number one hit "Beautiful." A followup album, *Back to Basics*, was released four years later. *Back to Basics* was nominated for a Grammy for Best Pop Vocal Album.

## MORE THAN A SINGER

Although Aguilera is best known for her work as a singer, she is also an active philanthropist. One of the charities she supports is the Women's Center and Shelter of Greater Pittsburgh, an

organization in Christina's hometown that provides support to women affected by domestic violence.

The young singer has also worked to help victims of Hurricane Katrina. When she married husband Jordan Bratman in 2005, she donated all of her wedding gifts to Katrina victims.

Another cause Aguilera contributes to regularly is the fight against acquired immune deficiency syndrome (AIDS). She has worked as a spokesperson for the MAC AIDS Fund and as a contributor to various AIDS projects.

When Christina isn't singing or working with charitable causes, she spends time with her son, Max Liron Bratman. Aguilera married music executive Jordan Bratman in 2005. Their son, Max, was born in January 2008. Although she refers to her son as her "greatest song," she does plan to continue making music for years to come.

*Elton John and Aguilera perform at Radio City Music Hall, in New York City, at a 2006 fundraiser for the Elton John AIDS Foundation.*

## CHAPTER EIGHT

# Diana Taurasi: Basketball Star

Of Argentine and Italian heritage, Diana Taurasi is best known for her skill on the basketball court. Many people consider her to be one of the greatest college basketball players of all time. A number one pick in the Women's National Basketball Association (WNBA) draft, Taurasi plays for the Phoenix Mercury today. Her talent and dedication have earned her numerous awards and two Olympic gold medals.

## EARLY LIFE

Diana's father, Mario, was born in a very small village on the outskirts of Naples, Italy. When he was five years old, his family moved to Argentina. Many people from Italy have settled in Argentina. In fact, it is estimated that 60 to 70 percent of Argentina's population is of Italian descent.

When he was a young man, Mario met and later married an Argentine named Liliana. In 1980 they moved with their baby daughter Jessika to the United States. The family settled in Chino, a small suburb of Los Angeles.

Diana Lurena Taurasi was born not long after, on June 11, 1982, in Glendale. She and her sister Jessika grew up in a quiet neighborhood. Both of the girls were athletic and enjoyed playing a variety of sports.

Diana's favorite afterschool activity was basketball. She played every single day from afternoon until dark. Diana often challenged herself to see how far she could shoot and how many baskets she could make in a row. It wasn't long before the neighborhood boys were issuing their own basketball challenges. Diana says:

> I always liked playing against guys more than girls when I was growing up. They were bigger and stronger, so I had to be smarter, be a better shooter, be a better passer and know how to rebound better. I loved the challenge of playing them one-on-one.

## BIG DREAMS

By the seventh grade, Diana was dreaming of using her skills on the basketball court to earn a scholarship to college. She worked hard on her game and became better and better. It was no surprise when Diana earned a spot as a starting player on the basketball

team of Don Lugo High School during her freshman year. She averaged 35.7 points that year.

Taurasi continued to play throughout her high school years. By the end of her senior year, she had a high school career total of 3,047 points. Because of her record she was named the 2000 Naismith Female Prep National Player of the Year. Other recognition included being named *Parade Magazine*'s All-American and receiving the 2000 Cheryl Miller Award, given by the *Los Angeles Times* to the best high school player in southern California.

The young basketball star also drew the attention of college recruiters and coaches. They came to Don Lugo often to watch Diana play. Many

*Women's National Basketball star Diana Taurasi of the Phoenix Mercury drives to the basket during a September 14, 2008, game against the Indiana Fever.*

Diana Taurasi: Basketball Star

of them were hoping she would join their basketball team. During her senior year, Diana received so many phone calls and offers from recruiters that she had to hide at a friend's house just so she could get her homework done.

## UCLA VS. UCONN

Sifting through college options during her senior year was tough, but Diana eventually narrowed down her choices to two schools: University of California at Los Angeles (UCLA) and the University of Connecticut (UConn). She thought the University of Connecticut had a better basketball program, but UCLA was much closer to Chino, where the Taurasis lived. Diana's mother encouraged her daughter to choose UCLA and stay close to home.

Diana has stated on several occasions that the heritage of UConn's coach, Geno Auriemma, played a role in her decision. He was born in Italy, in a village just a few miles away from the town where Diana's father, Mario, came from. During the coach's visits to the Taurasi family, the two men traded stories in Italian and talked about their experiences as immigrants to the United States. Auriemma eventually convinced the Taurasi family that UConn was the best school for Diana.

◄ CROSS-CURRENTS ►

To read more about how Diana Taurasi helps celebrate her Hispanic heritage, turn to page 55.

## THE HUSKIES

Diana began playing with the UConn Huskies during the 2000–2001 season. She did well as a freshman and even better as a sophomore. Her dedication and experience with one-on-one games had made her an amazing basketball player. In her sophomore year, Diana's coach, Auriemma, told reporters that her talent was unrivaled:

*Taurasi cuts down the net after the UConn Huskies defeat the Tennessee Lady Volunteers in the NCAA women's championship game on April 8, 2003, in Atlanta, Georgia.*

Nobody can guard Diana one-on-one going to the basket. She's so good that she's made me rethink how we do things in our offense. By the time she leaves here she can be the greatest player in the history of the women's college game. She has a lot of work to do, but the potential is certainly there.

And Taurasi did live up to her potential. During her time at UConn she helped the team win 139 of the 147 games in which she played. And she helped lead the Huskies to three consecutive National Collegiate Athletic Association (NCAA) championships. Among the many awards Diana won during her years as a college player were the Wade Trophy, the Big East College Player of the Year Award, the Associated Press Player of the Year Award, and the Naismith College Player of the Year Award. She even received a nomination for state heroine from Senator Thomas Gaffey.

*Taurasi sports her second gold medal, earned as a member of the U.S. Women's Senior National Team at the 2008 Olympics, held in Beijing, China.*

## WNBA ALL-STAR

In April 2004—a month before she was to graduate—Diana was the number one pick in the WNBA draft. She was selected by the Phoenix Mercury, based in Arizona.

Two months later Taurasi was also chosen to represent the United States as a member of the women's national basketball team at the 2004 Olympics being held that summer in Athens, Greece. At 22 years old, Diana was the youngest player on the team. She played well and helped the United States bring home the gold medal that August.

The summer of 2004 was also Taurasi's first season with the Phoenix Mercury. By the end of the regular season, in September, she had averaged 17 points per game. Her performance earned her the WNBA's Rookie of the Year Award. She was also named to the Western Conference All-Star team.

Taurasi continued to show she was an asset for her team. After her second season with the Phoenix Mercury, she was again selected to play for the West in the WNBA All-Star game. The following year, in 2006, she became the first WNBA player to break the 800-point mark in a single season.

In 2007 Taurasi helped the Phoenix Mercury take home the WNBA championship title. That win made Diana the sixth player in WNBA history to earn an NCCA title, an Olympic gold medal, and a WNBA title.

In August 2008 Taurasi earned a second Olympic gold medal at the Beijing Games. And she excelled for the Phoenix Mercury during the 2008 season, too, averaging 24.1 points per game. That September she received the WNBA Peak Performer for 2008 award for being the league's leading scorer. At the top of her game, Diana Taurasi can look forward to many more years of success.

## ATTITUDES TOWARD IMMIGRATION

The Gallup Organization surveys people around the world to determine public opinion regarding various political, social, and economic issues. One issue that Gallup has researched over the years is immigration to the United States. In general, Americans have a positive view of immigration, reports the Gallup Web site:

> Three in four [Americans] have consistently said it has been good for the United States in the past, and a majority says it is good for the nation today. However, Americans still seem interested in limiting the amount of immigration.

When asked in a July 2008 Gallup survey about the level of immigration into the United States, 39 percent of Americans favored decreasing the number of immigrants allowed into the country, a decrease from 45 percent a year earlier. However, only 18 percent believe it should be increased.

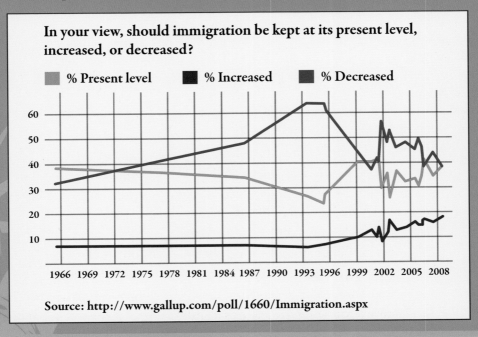

In your view, should immigration be kept at its present level, increased, or decreased?

■ % Present level    ■ % Increased    ■ % Decreased

Source: http://www.gallup.com/poll/1660/Immigration.aspx

## RAFAEL PELLI: GREEN ARCHITECT

Cesar isn't the only architect in the Pelli family. His son Rafael is also an accomplished designer. Rafael earned a bachelor of arts degree from Yale University in 1978 before joining his father's architectural firm in 1979. Two years later he went back to school to earn a master's degree from Harvard University.

Rafael went to work for Cesar Pelli and Associates again in 1989. He helped to design a number of the firm's prize-winning projects and was made the head of the firm's New York office in 2000. Five years later Cesar made his son Rafael and his colleague Fred Clarke partners. Cesar Pelli and Associates was renamed Pelli Clarke Pelli Architects.

Rafael Pelli is a member of the United States Green Building Council, a non-profit organization that works to make "green" buildings available to everyone. Green buildings are more energy efficient than other buildings and cause less damage to the environment. Rafael lectures on the importance of green building at universities all over the country. He also incorporates the green approach into project designs whenever possible.

## THE CHILEAN COUP OF 1973

In 1970 the cousin of Isabel's father, Salvador Allende, was elected president of Chile. He was the country's first socialist president. As he introduced socialist policies, such as the government takeover of foreign-owned industries, Allende was regarded with hostility by officials for the U.S. government.

General Augusto Pinochet led the military coup, funded and supported by the CIA, that took place on September 11, 1973. Salvador Allende refused to give in to the rebellion and resign the presidency. Although nobody knows for sure what happened next—the military claimed he committed suicide—it is assumed that he was assassinated on the night of September 11. The coup ushered in a military dictatorship that would span two decades.

General Augusto Pinochet declared himself president immediately afterwards and began to take control of the country. He implemented harsh measures against all who opposed him. Over the next 15 years, tens of thousands of Chileans were tortured and imprisoned under the regime. Three thousand people either "went missing" or were killed.

Like other writers and intellectuals of the time, Isabel expressed her outrage publicly. She helped others find their way out of the country until she was forced to flee to Venezuela with her family as well. Pinochet's reign ended in 1990, but he was never punished for his abuses of basic human rights.

## ELDY BANDA: QUECHUA NATIVE AMERICAN ACTIVIST

During the 1960s and 1970s Eldy Banda was a dedicated Native American activist. Benjamin Bratt has said that it was his mother's excitement and activism that taught him to be adventurous, as well as appreciate his Amerindian heritage. He told one interviewer, "When we were kids she would pack us into the car and drive us all over the South-west to different powwows. She was a very freewheeling, free-spirited woman, and that's a gift she gave to all us kids."

In 1969 Eldy took five-year-old Benjamin and his siblings to a protest held at Alcatraz, an abandoned federal prison in the San Francisco Bay. The protest had been organized by the American Indian Movement (AIM), which sought to bring attention to the problems of poverty and poor education faced by Native Americans in the United States.

Eldy Banda and her children arrived at the protest the day after it began. During the 19-month-long AIM demonstration Eldy, Benjamin, and the rest of the family slept at the prison two to three nights a week over the course of more than a year. The U.S. government ended the protest by force on June 11, 1971.

## U.S. CITIZENSHIP

Like many immigrants, Bob Burnquist has dual citizenship. Also known as dual nationality, dual citizenship means a person is recognized as a citizen of two different nations. Bob is a citizen of Brazil, the country of his birth. He is also a citizen of the United States because his father was a U.S. citizen.

Every country has different citizenship laws and policies. Not every country allows dual citizenship. In fact, there are some countries that discourage people from being citizens of multiple nations. To become a U.S. citizen, you must:

Be born in the United States
Be the child of a U.S. citizen
Voluntarily become a citizen through naturalization

Most immigrants become a U.S. citizen through naturalization. To become a naturalized citizens in the United States, immigrants must meet certain criteria: A foreign-born immigrant must have lived continuously in the United States for a minimum of five years. He or she must also be a lawful, permanent resident who is over the age of 18 and has passed a citizenship exam.

People who are dual citizens of the United States and a foreign country have the rights given to citizens of both nations. In the United States, citizens have the right to vote and the right to bring other family members to the United States. They also have the right to become elected officials.

# ENGLISH LANGUAGE LEARNERS

**W**ilmer Valderrama did not know how to speak English when he arrived in the United States. His situation is more common than most people think. Many of the families who immigrate to the United States have children who do not speak English. The Department of Education estimates that one out of every ten kids in U.S. public schools cannot speak fluent English. These students are known as ELLs (English Language Learners.)

The number of ELL students in the United States is expected to double in the next 20 years. As a result many school systems have to decide how to best meet the needs of ELL students. Some schools provide English as a Second Language (ESL) programs in which instruction in the students' native language is given and English is taught at the same time. Other schools provide bilingual education, which means that ELL students and English-speaking students are taught in two different languages. This method is becoming very popular in U.S. schools.

Because immigrants to the United States come from all over the world, it is difficult to develop programs that work for everyone. According to the U.S. Department of Education, ELL students speak more than 460 different languages. Spanish and Asian languages are the most common. But if schools use these languages alone, there are many ELL students who would be excluded.

*A teacher helps the members of an elementary school reading group.*

## CHRISTINA AGUILERA'S *MI REFLEJO*

According to a Gallup poll conducted in 2001, 26 percent of American adults are able to speak another language in addition to English. Nearly 55 percent of these people speak Spanish. Until recently, Christina Aguilera was not one of them. Although her father was from Ecuador and her mother was a Spanish interpreter, she didn't grow up speaking Spanish. In the late 1990s, she decided she should learn.

Aguilera had a basic understanding of the language, but she wasn't fluent enough to sing or converse in Spanish. She worked hard to improve her vocabulary, though, and was able to record an entire album in Spanish.

The album consisted of five songs from her self-titled debut album and five original numbers. Aguilera called the album *Mi Reflejo,* which translates to "My Reflection" in English. *Mi Reflejo* was released in 2000.

*Mi Reflejo* sold more than 3 million copies worldwide and produced two chart-topping singles. The album eventually went on to win a Latin Grammy Award for Best Female Pop Vocal Album. The win made Aguilera the first American artist to ever be honored with a Latin Grammy.

## NATIONAL HISPANIC HERITAGE MONTH

Diana is very proud of her Latin heritage. She celebrates Hispanic Heritage Month every year and has participated in several campaigns with the WNBA to encourage other people to do the same. Hispanic Heritage Month is a monthlong event that celebrates Hispanic heritage and culture. It also pays tribute to the contributions that Hispanic Americans have made to the United States.

America begins celebrating Hispanic Heritage Month on September 15 every year. The celebration ends 30 days later on October 15. The dates are no accident. This time period has special meaning to people of Latin descent. September 15 is the anniversary of the day in 1821 that five Latin American countries (Costa Rica, El Salvador, Guatemala, Honduras, and Nicaragua) declared independence. September 16 is the day people in Mexico celebrate their country's independence, and September 18 is when people in Chile celebrate theirs.

# NOTES

## CHAPTER 2

p. 13: "I don't feel I'm . . ." Kurt Andersen, "Big Yet Still Beautiful: In Today's Cityscapes, Cesar Pelli's Buildings Are Like Dancers Among Thugs," *Time* (September 24, 1990), 98.

p. 15: "I came east without . . ." Andersen, "Big Yet Still Beautiful: In Today's Cityscapes, Cesar Pelli's Buildings Are Like Dancers Among Thugs," 98.

## CHAPTER 3

p. 19: "From the moment we . . ." Isabel Allende, *My Invented Country: A Nostalgic Journey Through Chile* (New York: HarperCollins, 2003), 78.

p. 20: "After the military coup . . ." Isabel Allende, "Questions and Answers," Isabel Allende, 2008. http://www.isabelallende.com/curious_frame.htm

p. 22: "That book was written . . ." Isabel Allende, "Questions and Answers." http://www.isabelallende.com/curious_frame.htm

## CHAPTER 4

p. 25: "She made us aware . . ." Brendan Lemon, "Benjamin Bratt," *Interview* (May 2000), 122.

## CHAPTER 5

p. 30: "There's a wide gap . . ." Bob Burnquist and Matt Higgins, "Ramped Up: Skateboarding Changed Bob Burnquist's Life. Now He Is Changing Skateboarding." *Sports Illustrated for Kids* (August 1, 2002), 27.

p. 30: "Skateboarding snapped me out . . ." Burnquist and Higgins, "Ramped Up."

p. 31: "One thing led to . . ." "What About Bob?" *Official U.S. Playstation Magazine* (September 1, 2003).

p. 33: "I'll probably be on . . ." Burnquist and Higgins, "Ramped Up."

## CHAPTER 6

p. 36: "Just picture a kid . . ." Tom Gliatto and Ulrica Wihlborg, "Show Time: Wilmer Valderrama from Venezuela Speaks Fluent Sitcom on That '70s Show," *People Weekly* (September 10, 2001), 119.

p. 37: "If it weren't for them . . ." Gliatto and Wihlborg, "Show Time."

p. 39: "The name Calavena comes from . . ." "Star Maps: Wilmer Valderrama and Calavena," *Nylon*, August 28, 2007. http://www.nylonmag.com/?parid=426&section=article

## CHAPTER 7

p. 42: "I constantly felt like . . ." Dennis Hensley, "Christina Up Close," *The Advocate* (September 12, 2006), 46.

p. 44: "This album was about . . ." Cyndi Lauper, "Christina Aguilera: Keep Watching, She's a Work in Progress," *Interview* (August 2003), 113.

## CHAPTER 8

p. 47: "I always liked playing . . ." Quoted in Lars Anderson, "The Next Big Thing: For Diana Taurasi, Blessed with the Most Unstoppable One-on-One Game in Women's Hoops, the Best Is Yet to Come," *Sports Illustrated* (April 11, 2002), 58.

p. 49: "Nobody can guard Diana . . ." Quoted in Anderson, "The Next Big Thing."

## CROSS-CURRENTS

p. 53: "When we were kids . . ." Laura Jamison, "Benjamin Bratt," *InStyle* (May 1, 1999), 139.

# GLOSSARY

**Amerindian**—indigenous peoples of the Americas; American Indian.

**colonize**—to establish a colony, which is a region under the political control of another country's government.

**coup**—a violent or forced overthrow of an existing government.

**descendant**—a person who comes from a specific ancestor.

**diplomat**—an official who represents a government in relationships with a foreign country's government.

**emigrant**—a person who moves away from his or her country to settle in another country or region.

**exile**—a state of forced separation from one's country or home.

**fictional**—something that is invented or untrue; something that comes from the imagination.

**Grammy**—an annual award given by the National Academy of Recording Arts and Sciences for outstanding achievement in the recording industry.

**immigrant**—a person who comes to live in a new country or region.

**indigenous**—native to a specific place.

**interpreter**—an individual who translates languages.

**Latin America**—the parts of the Americas where the national language is Latin-based, especially Spanish and Portuguese. Latin America includes countries in South America and Central America, as well as the country of Mexico.

**naturalized citizen**—a person who has officially acquired the rights of nationality in a country after being born somewhere else.

**poll**—a survey, often conducted over the phone, in person or over the Internet, in which the public's attitudes toward specific issues are documented.

**Quechua**—an indigenous people of South America; also, the language spoken by the Quechua people.

**refugee**—an individual who is forced to flee a country to remain safe.

**restaurateur**—an individual who owns or operates restaurants.

**unorthodox**—contrary to what is usual; non-traditional.

# FURTHER READING

Aguilera, Christina. *Christina Aguilera: Back to Basics*. Milwaukee: Hal Leonard Corporation, 2007.

Allende, Isabel. *The Sum of Our Days: A Memoir*. New York: HarperCollins, 2008.

Blohm, Judith and Terri Lapinsky. *Kids Like Me: Voices of the Immigrant Experience*. Boston: Intercultural Press, 2006.

Goodfellow, Evan. *Skateboarding: Ramp Tricks*. Chula Vista: Tracks Publishing, 2006.

Greenberger, Robert. *Christina Aguilera*. New York: Rosen Publishing Group, 2008.

Janer, Zilkia. *Latino Food Culture*. West Port: Greenwood Publishing Group, 2008.

Karmel, Terese. *Hoop Tales: UConn Huskies Women's Basketball*. Guilford: Globe Pequot Press, 2005.

Pelli, Cesar and Michael Crosbie. *Petronas Towers: The Architecture of High Construction*. Hoboken: Wiley, John & Sons, Incorporated, 2005.

# INTERNET RESOURCES

http://www.bobburnquist.com
The official Web site of Bob Burnquist showcases videos, photos, news, and information about Bob and his sponsors. Visitors can view the site in English or Portuguese.

http://www.cesar-pelli.com
Cesar Pelli's official Web site offers information about his architectural firm and includes an image gallery of Pelli's past projects.

http://www.christinaaguilera.com
Fans of Christina Aguilera can learn more about the singer on her official Web site, which includes a bio, news, photos, tour dates, forums, and a free music player.

http://www.dianataurasi.com
Diana Taurasi's official Web site lets fans follow Diana's progress via news releases and an online journal. It also links to basketball stats, camp and event information, and photos.

http://www.gallup.com
Gallup provides 70 years of research information on the organization's Web site.

http://www.isabelallende.com
Isabel Allende's official Web site features a detailed bio, information about Allende's books, links to speeches and interviews, family photos, and much more.

# OTHER SUCCESSFUL AMERICANS OF SOUTH AMERICAN HERITAGE

**Luis Aparicio (1934– ):** The son of a notable Venezuelan baseball player, Luis Ernesto Aparicio Montiel was born in Maracaibo, Venezuela. The former shortstop in professional baseball (1956–1973) is widely considered to be one of the 100 greatest baseball players of all time. He was the first South American native to be honored with an induction into the Baseball Hall of Fame.

**Morena Baccarin (1979– ):** Born in Rio de Janeiro, Brazil, Morena Baccarin immigrated to the United States when she was only 10 years old. She began her professional acting career in 2001 and has since appeared in several popular movies and television shows.

**Jordana Brewster (1980– ):** Born in 1980 in Panama City, Panama, Brewster spent time in London and her mother's native Brazil before moving to the United States at the age of 10. Five years later, she made her acting debut on a daytime soap opera. She has since appeared in a number of movies and television shows.

**Ariel Dorfman (1942– ):** Born in Buenos Aires, Argentina, in 1942, Dorfman is an accomplished novelist, playwright, journalist, and human rights activist. He served as a cultural advisor to Salvador Allende before being forced to leave Chile in 1973. Dorfman became a United States citizen in 2004.

**Jaime Escalante (1930– ):** Born in Bolivia in 1930, mathematics teacher Jaime Escalante moved to the United States in 1964. He learned to speak English and went on to teach calculus in East Los Angeles. Escalante's work with minority students garnered nationwide attention and inspired several books and a movie.

**Alberto Fuget (1964– ):** Born Alberto Fuguet de Goyeneche in Santiago, Chile, in 1964, Fuget is an accomplished writer and film director who moved to California at the age of 13. His work has received wide acclaim in both Chile and the United States. In 1999 he was named one of the 50 most important Latin Americans for the new millennium by *Time* magazine.

*The daughter of Brazilian model Maria Joao Leal de Sousa, actress Jordana Brewster starred in the 2001 action thriller* The Fast and the Furious *and the 2004 comedy* D.E.B.S.

**Fernando Alvaro Lamas (1915–1982):** Latin movie star Fernando Alvaro Lamas y de Santos was born in Buenos Aires, Argentina, in 1915. He immigrated to the United States in 1951 and went on to star in and direct a number of movies and television shows.

**Carlos Llamosa (1969– ):** Born in 1969 in Palmira, Colombia, renowned soccer player Carlos Llamosa emigrated to the United States in 1991 to live with the rest of his family. He began playing professional soccer again in 1995 and became a naturalized U.S. citizen in 1998.

**Carmen Miranda (1909–1959):** Born in a small Portuguese town, Maria do Carmo Miranda da Cunha, later known as Carmen Miranda, moved to Brazil shortly after her birth. She became famous for promoting Brazil through her singing and acting. In the 1940s, she embarked on a career in North America and actively helped the U.S. government strengthen ties between the United States and Latin America.

**Carlos Noriega (1959– ):** Born in Lima, Peru, in 1959, Noriega moved to the United States as a child and went on to become a U.S. Marine Corps lieutenant colonel and a NASA astronaut. He has walked in space three times and has orbited the earth nearly 150 times.

**Horatio Sanz (1969– ):** Born in Santiago, Chile, in 1969, Horatio Sanz grew up in Chicago, Illinois. In 1998 he become the first Latino to join the cast of the popular television show *Saturday Night Live*. He has also appeared in several film comedies.

*Carlos I. Noriega, who flew on two NASA shuttle missions, in 1997 and 2000, has logged more than 480 hours in space.*

**Pancho Segura (1921– ):** Born Francisco Olegario Segura in Guayaquil, Ecuador, Pancho Segura moved to the United States in the late 1930s. He was a top-ranked tennis player in the 1940s and 1950s and was inducted into the International Tennis Hall of Fame in 1984.

**Nick Verreos (1967– ):** Born in Missouri in 1967 to a Greek-American father and a Venezuelan mother, Nick Verreos spent his childhood in Venezuela, where his great-great uncle was president. At the age of 10 Verreos moved to the United States, where he later established a career as a successful fashion designer.

# INDEX

Numbers in **bold italics** refer to captions.

# PICTURE CREDITS

# ABOUT THE AUTHOR

Karen Schweitzer has written numerous articles for magazines and newspapers, such as the *Erickson Tribune* and *Learning Through History*, and for Web sites like About.com. She is also the author of several books, including biographies for Shaun White, Tyra Banks, Soulja Boy Tell 'Em, and Sheryl Swoopes. You can learn more about Karen at www.karenschweitzer.com.